OCEAN

Food Webs

By William Anthony

Published in 2021 by
KidHaven Publishing, an Imprint of Greenhaven Publishing, LLC
353 3rd Avenue
Suite 255
New York, NY 10010

Edited by: Madeline Tyler
Designed by: Jasmine Pointer

Find us on

Cataloging-in-Publication Data

Names: Anthony, William.
Title: Ocean food webs / William Anthony.
Description: New York : KidHaven Publishing, 2021. | Series: Food webs | Includes glossary and index.
Identifiers: ISBN 9781534535282 (pbk.) | ISBN 9781534535305 (library bound) | ISBN 9781534535299 (6 pack) | ISBN 9781534535312 (ebook)
Subjects: LCSH: Marine ecology--Juvenile literature. | Marine plants--Juvenile literature. | Marine animals--Juvenile literature. | Food chains (Ecology)--Juvenile literature.
Classification: LCC QH541.5.S3 A584 2021 | DDC 577.7--dc23

Printed in the United States of America

CPSIA compliance information: Batch #BS20K. For further information contact Greenhaven Publishing LLC, New York, New York at 1-844-317-7404.

Please visit our website, www.greenhavenpublishing.com. For a free color catalog of all our high-quality books, call toll free 1-844-317-7404 or fax 1-844-317-7405.

CONTENTS

Words that look like **THIS** can be found in the glossary on page 24.

UNDER THE SEA

If you were to take a look at life under the sea, do you know what you might discover?

There are lots of different animals and plants to be found, all going about their daily business, and each and every one of them has a place in the food web.

Let's look at who eats who in the ocean. We're diving into cold waters for this one... Brr!

THE FOOD WEB

It all starts with the sun's energy...

...*HERBIVORES* eat the plants...

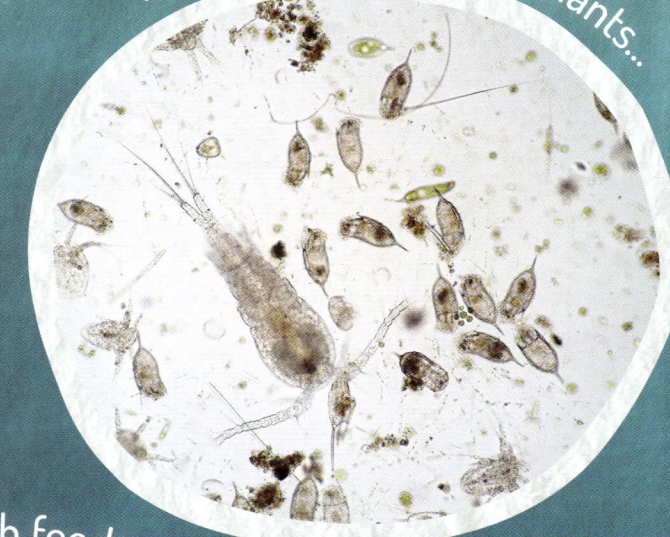

...which feeds plants...

...**CARNIVORES** eat the herbivores...

...and **APEX PREDATORS** eat those.

...bigger **PREDATORS** eat them...

THE ORCA

Move out of my way! I'm an orca, and I'm an apex predator. That means nobody will be eating me anytime soon. I'm happy to **STUN** a fish with my tail or grab a seal from the ice for my lunch.

NAME:	Orca
TYPE:	MAMMAL
HOME:	All Oceans
FOOD:	Carnivore
PREDATOR OR PREY?	Apex Predator

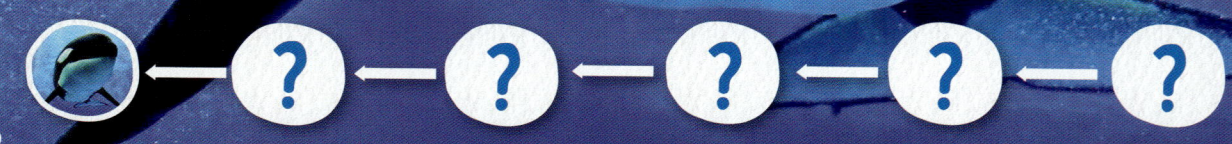

Seal: speedy but satisfying...?

Sea turtle: tough but tasty...?

Humpback whale: huge... but I'm hungry...?

Actually, sea lion is what I want. My POD and I will work together to make sure we have a delicious meal!

WHAT—OR WHO—IS FOR LUNCH?

9

THE SEA LION

Arf! Arf! Phew! I hid, and thankfully he's gone. I'm a sea lion, and that orca wanted me for his lunch! If he comes back, I'll have to swim as fast as I can—I'm faster than he is, but he's sneaky. By the way, all this talk of lunch has made me hungry...

NAME:	Sea Lion
TYPE:	Mammal
HOME:	Pacific Ocean
FOOD:	Carnivore
PREDATOR OR PREY?	Both

Shhh! Don't make a sound...

Sardines: crunchy but satisfying...?

Squid: squishy but tasty...?

Salmon: my favorite... but hard to catch...?

No, no, those just won't do. What I really want for lunch is...

TURN THE PAGE! QUICK!

THE HERRING

Swim away as fast as you can—there's a sea lion on our tails! Thankfully, there are lots of us in our <u>SHOAL</u>. If we stick together, it's more difficult for that pesky sea lion to catch us. There are predators everywhere hoping to gulp us down for their lunch!

NAME:	Herring
TYPE:	Fish
HOME:	All Oceans
FOOD:	<u>OMNIVORE</u>
PREDATOR OR PREY?	Both

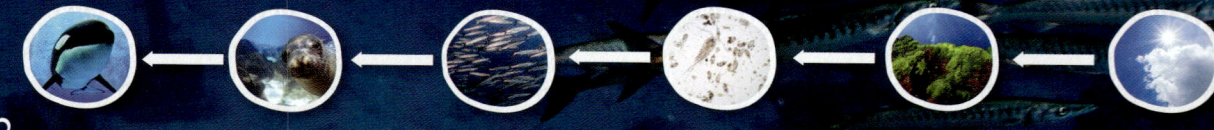

My favorite meal is plankton. Luckily for me, it's floating around everywhere! There are lots of my friends who are trying to get the best bits too, so I'd better swim as fast as I can to beat them to it...

Phytoplankton (say: FIE-toe-plank-ton): tasty, tiny plants...?

Krill: pretty in pink...?

Zooplankton: tasty, tiny animals...?

Hmm. I can't decide. Maybe I'll just eat all of them! Hang on... is that a seal?

QUICK! HIDE!

THE LEOPARD SEAL

Ooomph! Those little fish are tough to catch! With a flick of my flippers, I can dive down into deep water or get up enough speed to catch up with them—but not today. I'll have to have something else...

NAME:	Leopard Seal
TYPE:	Mammal
HOME:	Antarctica
FOOD:	Carnivore
PREDATOR OR PREY?	Both

Now then, what do I want for lunch today?

Krill: A yummy winter meal...?

Small seals: Hard work to catch...?

Squid: a tentacled treat...?

Hang on... what's that sound? I think I hear a penguin. My favorite!

LET'S GO SEE!

THE EMPEROR PENGUIN

Is that leopard seal gone? I may be the biggest of all the penguins, but I'm no match for those snapping jaws! Anyway, I can't stop to chat—I've got to eat as much as I can before I go back to look after the kids!

NAME:	Emperor Penguin
TYPE:	Bird
HOME:	Around Antarctica
FOOD:	Carnivore
PREDATOR OR PREY?	Both

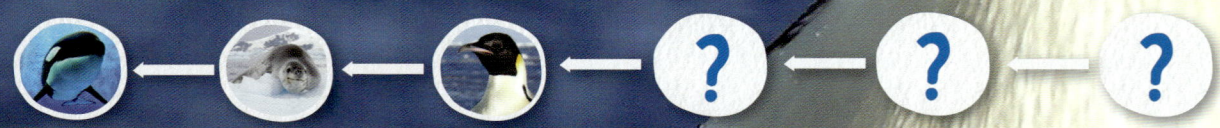

Now then, what's on the menu today?

Shhh! Don't tell the penguin I'm here!

Herring: a hearty meal...?

Squid: satisfying but stringy...?

No, no... I want an old favorite today, and there's always plenty of it around...

WHAT COULD IT BE?

THE KRILL

I might be tiny, but I am pretty mighty! Krill are a keystone species—this means that we are VERY important. So many things like to eat us that, if we weren't here, the whole food web could fall apart!

NAME:	Krill
TYPE:	CRUSTACEAN
HOME:	All Oceans
FOOD:	Omnivore
PREDATOR OR PREY?	Both

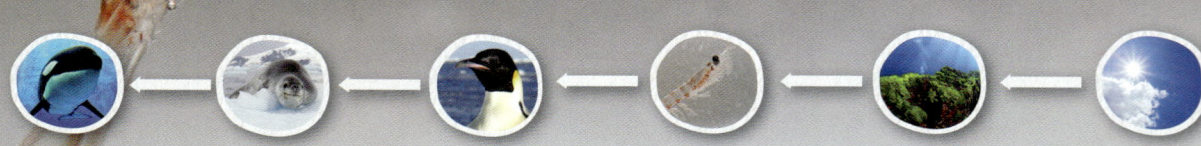

I'm so small, I can only eat really tiny things...

Zooplankton: teeny tiny animals...?

Phytoplankton: teeny tiny plants...?

Algae: got to get your greens...?

Wait a minute...
what's that under the water...?

LOOK OUT!

19

THE HUMPBACK WHALE

GULP! Yum–yum, a huge mouthful of tasty krill and plankton for me! Delicious! I don't have any teeth, but I'm really big, so I just take a gulp of water and filter out the food! Krill, plankton... I'm not picky!

NAME:	Humpback Whale
TYPE:	Mammal
HOME:	All Oceans
FOOD:	Carnivore
PREDATOR OR PREY?	Both

I've got such a big mouth, I can eat over 5,500 pounds (2,500 kg) of krill each day!

Eventually, the sun's energy makes its way through the food web to every living thing in the ocean.

OCEAN FOOD WEB

The arrows follow where the energy goes. Can you follow the energy from the sun all the way to the orca?

SEAL

SEA LION

ORCA

PENGUIN

SEA TURTLE

SQUID

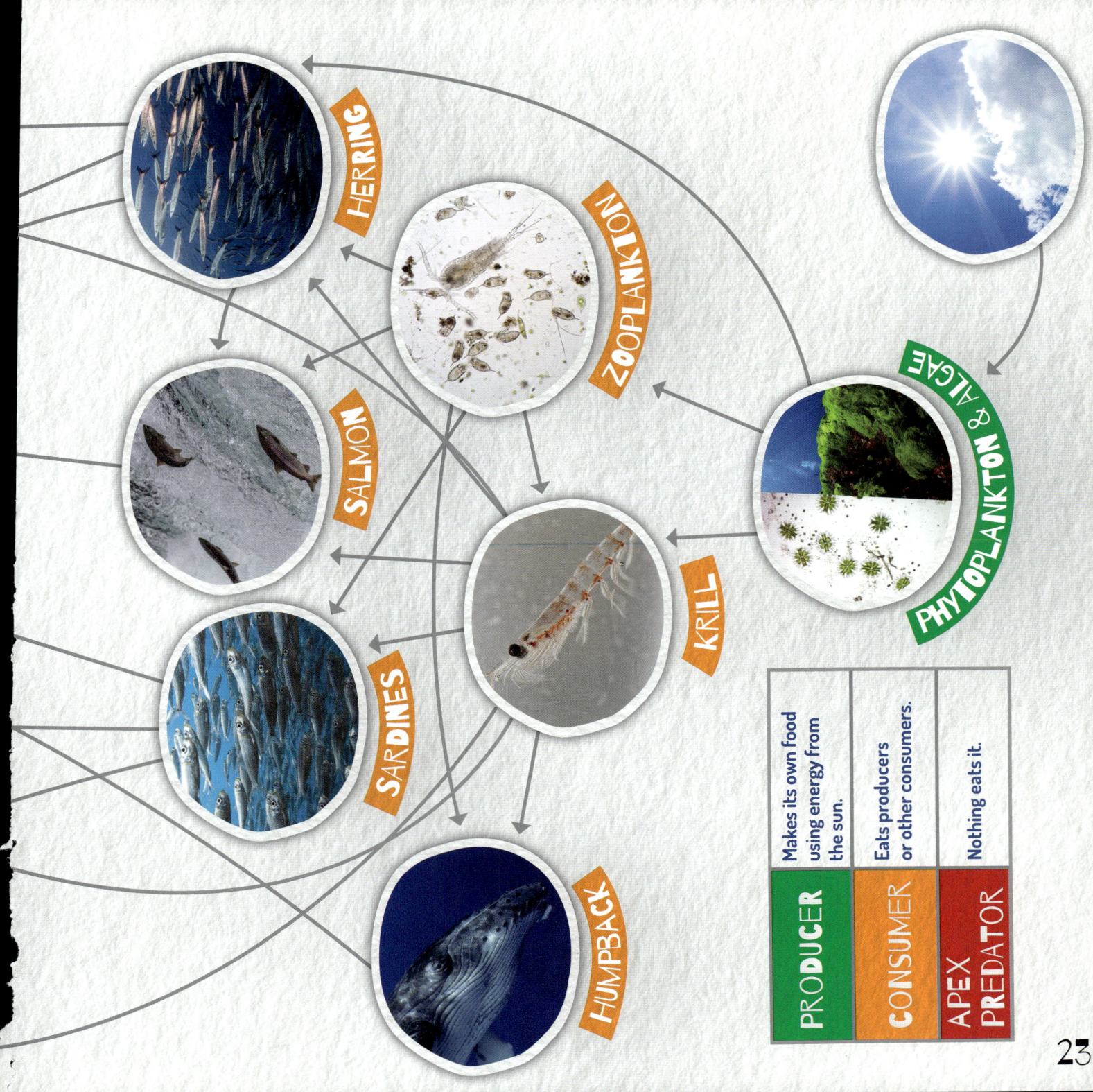

HERRING

ZOOPLANKTON

PHYTOPLANKTON & ALGAE

SALMON

KRILL

SARDINES

HUMPBACK

PRODUCER	Makes its own food using energy from the sun.
CONSUMER	Eats producers or other consumers.
APEX PREDATOR	Nothing eats it.

GLOSSARY

apex predator   The top predator in a food chain, with no natural predators of its own.

carnivore   An animal that eats other animals instead of plants.

crustacean   An animal that lives in water and has a hard outer shell.

herbivore   An animal that eats plants instead of other animals.

mammal   An animal that has warm blood, a backbone, and produces milk.

omnivore   An animal that eats both plants and other animals.

pod   A group of whales that are bonded, either as family or friends.

predator   An animal that hunts other animals for food.

prey   Animals that are hunted for food.

shoal   A large group of the same kind of fish.

stun   To make something become unconscious.

INDEX